Butterfly

Butterfly

A Poem Sequence by Diane Kerr

Cherry Grove Collections

Published by Cherry Grove Collections
P.O. Box 541106
Cincinnati, OH 45254-1106

ISBN: 9781625490810
LCCN: 2014936224

Poetry Editor: Kevin Walzer
Business Editor: Lori Jareo

Visit us on the web at www.cherry-grove.com

Acknowledgements

Some of the segments in this sequence were published as a chapbook by Parallel Press in 2006.

The following segments of this sequence, some in slightly altered forms, have appeared in these publications:

Alaska Quarterly Review: segments beginning with the first lines:

> "At thirty thousand feet, two moons"
> "Halved and huge, a cut blood orange"
> "I was at the clinic, between patients"
> "It's a mistake to believe"
> "Banker one, still can't balance"

The Diagram: the segment from Section I,
Sistering, which begins:
> "Early September: fall is proceeding"

> Segments from Section III, *Little Thief,*
which begin:
> "White winter sky blurring into white land,"
> "Once, a gladness,"
> "World champions, he holds"
> "Morning was sunning the deck"
> "Last night I dreamed him prancing in the
aquamarine,"
> "Some poets want their tercets"
> "Inside of her"

The Pittsburgh Post Gazette: the segment from
Section II which begins:
> "Crouched under wrought-iron frets"

The poems that ultimately became this sequence began several months after my twin brother's death, which occurred while I was in the middle of working on a MFA at the Warren Wilson Program for Writers. I owe a great debt of gratitude to my friends and teachers in the Warren Wilson community for their solace and expertise in helping me write what grief demanded I write. I was fortunate early on to have as supervising mentors the late Steve Orlen and Tony Hoagland who both encouraged me with skill and generosity. Ellen Bryant Voigt taught me the possibilities of the long sequence poem through Robert Penn Warren's *Audubon,* and Michael Ryan provided me the safest possible space to write through pain and close to the bone. In the years that followed, I've also been fortunate to have the support of Warren Wilson alumni through alumni conferences. In particular, Terri Ford and Anne McCrary Sullivan provided early and helpful manuscript feedback.

Before I pursued an MFA, after decades of not writing since adolescence, at age fifty I joined a women's writing workshop, *The Madwomen in the Attic* directed by the late Patricia Dobler under the auspices of Carlow University in Pittsburgh. Pat and the *Madwomen* welcomed me and supported my writing more than they will ever know. Molly Peacock was an early visiting consultant whose feedback on my work then, and years later on this manuscript, was essential. I continue to study and write with the *Madwomen* and deeply appreciate the support of Jan Beatty, present and stellar director, and workshops led by Joy Katz and Ellen McGrath Smith. Two *"Madwomen Emeriti,"* Carolyn Luck and M.J. Place, are cherished friends and have been unstinting champions of my work as has Rick St.

John.

I feel a great debt of the heart to my earliest mentors, two high school teachers: Marv Solomon who named me writer at fourteen and John Meyer who gave a lost girl refuge and a lifelong love of poetry.

I thank my husband, John McCall, for his love and unfaltering support and my daughter, Marie Lewis, for designing the cover. I am also grateful to Jon Spiegel, who has endured over the long haul, helping me to untangle the narratives of my childhood and thus heal and grow. I worked for many years as a child and family therapist. The children and families I served taught me lessons of suffering and strength I hope have informed this work.

In Memory of my Mother
Petrina J. Kerr
and my Brother
David H. Kerr

In order to sing, sadness
will have to drink black water.
—Jose' Luis Hidalgo
"Shore of Night"
Translated by Hardie St. Martin

The one who can sing sings to the one who can't,
who waits in the pit, like Procne among the slaves,
as the gods decide how all such stories end
—Ellen Bryant Voigt
"Song and Story"

Table of Contents

I

Sistering

Unsustainable silent weight
on the cross-beams, deep fissures
surfacing in the plaster.
The contractor said my house
was falling slowly inward;
some previous soul had removed
a load-bearing wall, some joists
were shorter than others, couldn't
support what they weren't made to support.

So he *sistered* them, which means
to splice, to add a sort of splint
that connects each inadequate
sagging side to the other, spanning
the weakness in the middle, making
the heaviness bearable again.

*

At thirty thousand feet, two moons
compete in the window view: one,
a high August chrysanthemum, the other
its wavering orange reflection
on the long sack of lake Michigan.

Again I will arrive, uninvited
to visit my drunken brother,
brother, from the Greek *phrater*—
as in fraternity, as in fratricide.
Always he swims away from me, always
kicking away; I was the dark moon
curled against him in the first sky
of the first night, curled crescent;
I was the always other.

How annoying another self
shadowing the barely self, brother,
as in brotherhood, next door
to brothel, Old English neighbor
of *breothan* which means to waste away,
to go to ruin. I mean to intrude.

The 737 slides its shadow
across the calm evening lake
and drones down to mild clear Milwaukee.
He was the expected, hoped-for one;
it was 1942, before sonograms.
Sometimes the two hearts beat together.

*

She's had two weeks warning, and long before,
she's had suspicions—eighty-pounds gained
on her 5'2" frame, throbbing swollen breasts
reaching down to her swollen belly bursting
with double her plan. One plants two feet
at the base of her spine, another
kicks a persistent staccato, both heads
press steadily up under her diaphragm—
she can't get comfortable, can't
even breathe lying down. So there she sits
through this long night, propped up
by pillows, sleeping husband young
as she is, stretched out beside her
heedless as an animal, and the crib

in the corner—she refuses to buy another,
says we can learn to share.
Second born herself of four in four years
before TB took her mother, how much
can she mother who wasn't much mothered?
We're already fighting it out
entangled inside her; elbows jabbing,
back to back we push each other away.

She fingers the itching stretch marks—
purple streaked with tiny red veins,
purled an inch wide down her sides—sighs,
shifts her sagging bulk and aching backbone
against the severe oak headboard.
Worry will keep her company, sit with her,
little Buddha under her Bodhi tree, waiting for us.

*

Stuff of family legend:

Every single time
we put her in that playpen,
he bit her! Round and
round they would go
until we rescued her.
It was so funny!

 Funny?
And just how many
rounds did it take?

*

She propped us up side by side,
tied us with knotted dishtowels
next to her on the front seat
of the green 37 Plymouth,
headed west, then northwest on 16, ticking
off the farm towns: Portage, Mauston,
Tomah, Black River Falls; in between—
empty March fields too frozen to work.
Augusta, Chippewa Falls, Cornell,
Sheldon, stopping once for gas, feeding,
changing. When one or the other cried,
she sang, or talked, or cried herself.
When we fell asleep, she reached
over, leaned us against each other.

Eight hours to Ladysmith, 10 miles more
on dirt to their godforsaken farm,
still without electricity, water
still hand-pumped, hauled
by bucket into the house,
stinking privy out behind the tool shed.

Husband staying home, busy
trying to get the business going.
Mother-in-law back there too
in tightlipped disapproval;
she went anyway, determined
to show her folks her twin babies, have
them see what she had made of herself.

*

Shared initials but not a rhyme,
no secret language, nearly nothing

from him for years. After awhile
I quit calling, quit sending cards.

Once, that pull of the moon,
he left a message: *Happy Birthday.*

That was it, not his name,
not *how are you, I love you too.*

It's my brother, I said.
How did I know? Ask the babies,

those preemie twins who survive better
in the same cramped incubator. Ask

what settles them, what calms
the small heaving lungs.

*

You were as caught as that five-year-old.
Late afternoon on a winter day
out playing alone in the snowdrifts
when your heavy woolen snowsuit
snagged on barbed wire. Flailing
and flailing in the falling light
until exhausted you hung there, silent,
tears freezing to your face.

When our mother found you,
she asked everyone the same question,

Why, why would he never call for me?

*

Thick fog and our headlights gone,
we're crossing the marshland
outside Pewaukee. Roy has already
leapt from galloping Trigger
onto the driverless stagecoach,
saving everyone.
                    Here, my uncle Jim,
newly graduated from high school,
is hanging far out the window into
the moist air, aiming a flashlight
onto the median for my mother.
She still believes and so do I.
Before we lost our lights,
we were singing *Rock of Ages,*
A Mighty Fortress, Come Thou
Almighty King, and the one
I'm learning in Children's Choir,
Now the Day is over.
                    1949,
big square station wagon,
wooden trim, worn red leather seats,
sounds of the low motor
and a host of jubilant spring peepers.
My brother and I are keeping watch
out the back window, staring
at the black of where we've been.
In three weeks Uncle Jim's seizures
will begin; now, he leans farther
into the fog, yells back,
We're okay, Pat, just keep her coming!

24

*

Halved and huge, a cut blood orange,
against the navy-blue sky the harvest moon
rose bruised, cross-hatched, flecked
with starlings swirling down to roost
on the wire veins of the city.

The earth and moon love each other
only once a year this way. Your life,
your only life, it was the moment I knew
your life was emptying from you.

Stub-tailed, speckled, ecstatic,
the starlings sang the world's beautiful song.

I stood in the parking lot and wept,
wept that you lay 600 miles away,
wept that you could neither hear
nor see the evening's old orange opera
and that you could no longer want to.

Nothing was garnered, gathered in,
and nothing was stored by.
They said you bled from every pore
and nothing, nothing could stanch it.

*

After everyone else gave up,
she persisted, taking an apple pie
or the elaborate custard torte he liked,
bringing it with pot roast, mashed potatoes,
all in separate little Tupperware containers.

She let herself in.
If he was up, they sat together.
Sometimes, he ate a bite or two.

The day she found him on the floor,
she called the ambulance
and waited by him, said she knew
this time he wouldn't make it.

Separate containers because
he never liked one food touching another.
She knew that. She always knew that.

*

I was at the clinic, between patients
when the receptionist buzzed me
and I went to the waiting room
and got my husband just as if
he were one of the children
and we walked back to my office
and I closed the door and I said
he's gone, isn't he? and my husband
nodded and kissed me, and I said
he's lost his life, he's lost his life
and sat down on the little orange chair
by the game shelf and the art shelf
and the people shelf of soldiers
and a clown and cowboys and a ballerina
and a bride and groom and a baseball team
by the sturdy wooden dollhouse where babies
have been eaten by starving dinosaurs
and stupid mean grown-ups have jumped
out windows into a deep lake of poop
and a giant tornado has come
and sucked out a whole family
and every stick of sturdy wooden furniture
and it's all fallen on top of them
in a big pile on the floor.

*

Hard white plaster helplessness—
the rest of that summer sullen
together—twins must be always
leaving and returning to a mirror.

I can't remember if I smashed
my elbow before or after he dove,
arms forward, through the hay chute
straight down. He must have seen
the milking-parlor floor coming:
lime-whitewashed bare cement.

It must have been after.
I was walking on a rolling barrel,
playing circus. I fell suddenly.
He didn't fall. He dove. Then
came walking slowly across the barnyard,
sleepwalker arms held out front, wrists
dangling limp, two hung things.
He came up the back steps as slowly
as in last night's nightmare.

But I fell quickly, backwards, surprised,
surprised as I was when the doctor
set the elbow—his sweet fruited
whiskey breath—and when he placed it,
the piercing inside crack of pain—

like that, it was like that
when you told me he was dead.

*

Behind the altar, evening has turned
the window of the sad-faced Jesus
and his two morose sheep a deep maroon.
We have walked down the red aisle
together at Uncle Jim's wedding, my hand
resting lightly as a moth on your arm.

Fifteen. You are a head taller,
white tux immaculate, blue carnation,
my dress blue-embroidered
white organza, blue taffeta sash.
In three years both of us
will marry. Your wonderful hair
smoothed to an almost pompadour,
grinning, you can't wait
to get back outside and finish
booby-trapping Uncle Jim's Chevrolet.

My braces finally gone, I'm smiling too,
my hair short, curled under a wreath
of dyed blue daisies. Below the puffed sleeve,
my crooked left elbow, touching yours.

*

Early September, fall is proceeding
as it is supposed to: the only purple,
asters in their appointed place
next to the only yellow, goldenrod
claiming the ditches.
Sumac is the only red—seeping
as it should, down the open hillsides.

If Spike were alive, expensive
dopey Spike, your big golden
who never got it right—
his one hunting season retrieving
lily-pad after lily-pad,
gleaming green tortillas
dripping from his big dumb mouth—
if Spike still lived, he would sniff
and get up for that family of geese
hustling south on schedule.

Leaves just begin to rust; green still holds.
A full month before Small Game begins,
the road-kill doe lies skewed, bloated
and tolerable: overhead the necessary ravens

scroll a black mandala on blue sky.
But on the shoulder of the road
stands a true vulture; sunlight slicks
the wine-red corrugated head—
too far north, too far north, never,
I've never seen one here before—
David, too soon—

How to bear the beak of disorder.

*

In one of eight twin pregnancies
one small creature forfeits,
becomes sacrificial, melts away
as if a mistake had been made.

A quiet erasure, an anomaly
called the *vanishing twin,*
brief shadow, eternal imprint.

No one can predict if this will happen,
nor how it happens, nor when, nor why.

II

First

Our mother's house
in the dream someone
a noise at the door
huge snarling Great Dane
rearing up, mouth open
I slam the door, know
it's going around
to the back yard where
the new puppy is playing
under the blooming lilacs
it has the puppy
snapping its neck again
and again then the puppy
is asleep on the summer lawn
I grab him I'm almost
to the back door, the Dane
is charging up the steps
I grab the hose, turn it on
fill the great mouth
its deep gullet enraged
it vomits lunges for us
I see the dark ridged pink
roof of its mouth,
I wake up.

Again you are dead.

*

The main rule is everybody has to look
in a different direction: the father
looks at the map flapping and blowing,
figures how many miles to Tucson; the mother
sits in the car, looks at the blackness

of her hands pressed hard on her eyes,
relives her mother's final faint, cries.
The boy lies on his belly, four feet
beyond the guard rail at the very edge
of the canyon rim, leans over, looks down

to the canyon floor, the quicksilver
river cutting its slender way out.
And the girl? Oh that drippy girl,
she can't find her own place to look—
that cheater looks at them all.

*

Milking time at the neighbor's farm.
From the far end of the pasture
the ever-nosy cows lumber in,
stand and watch, chewing their cuds
intent as ball players.

We hoist ourselves up for stolen rides
on the indulgent ones we know don't mind.
Our arms encircle their soft necks
and they walk us slowly around,
our legs stretching to straddle the huge bellies.

Each of us back inside the secret world,
we can do this with our eyes closed,
deep warmth seeping into our bodies.
From within, every here and there we feel
flutter kicks of their young.

*

Rank sour-green silage smell
hovering in the empty cement silo.
The more I beg him to stop
the higher he climbs,
doves clucking uneasily
around the top, metal rung
after rung he climbs
across shafts of dusty
light, not looking down
when he reaches the catwalk,
inching his way around
the narrow path, bumping
dove nests which fall,
shatter, almost soundlessly
into loose gray tangles.

He stands on tiptoe,
peers out a narrow vent,
surveys the quiet summer world,
then turns, looks down,
hangs on with one hand,
waves one leg, one arm:

Hey, Diane! Want me to jump?
Do you? Do you?

The dust floats,
settles out of the light.
I can see him clearly.

*

We didn't look alike.
Breech babies. *Two perfectly
round little heads,* our mother said,
though I outweighed him by a pound,
which worried her; she believed
only girls should be frail.
Her firstborn, both colicky,
he wasn't gaining. The doctor
gave him B-12 shots, the needle
so long when it plunged
into his small bottom,
she could hardly bear it.
When he died at fifty-four
she said, *Now my tiniest baby is gone.*

Only sometimes dressed alike,
blue sailor suit and sailor dress
the first day of kindergarten;
I was the frail one then.
Aren't they darling? the teachers mewed.
One put her thumb and index finger
around my wrist. *So thin! But she's
the smart one.* Another smiled, *Yes,
but he's the handsome one.*

We didn't look alike except
our eyes, the same hazel-green eyes.
When he appeared in the vision,
come back from eternal blackness

in the same piss-soaked bathrobe,
the same soft-clapping slippers
stuffed with his swollen mottled
ankles, ice cubes still rattling
in his glass, his face the same
yellow bruise, I looked into his eyes;
they were tear-filled, pleading.
They were my eyes.

*

You, the other twins, two
pairs of you our mother lost
before us, as though
her body practiced
twice before getting it right.

How appalled she was
at the thought of six.
And who can blame her—
six in three years.

I speak for us,
given the souls
your incompetent bodies
couldn't hold onto.
How sad you arrived
too soon to continue,
how sad that you left
all the continuance
to us, who are no longer us.

*

Crouched under wrought-iron frets
of our wooden desks, we wait
through grade school, practicing
disaster, the giant mushroom
that would foreclose our future.
Calamity has already come

to claim my brother,
held back in second grade.
When he isn't sitting
in the principal's office, he sits
scowling at the happy children
in the impossible reader.

I have gone on to third.
Regular drills down the rickety
iron fire escapes, each class a place
on the graveled playground, each child
a partner. Always I look for him,
always I make sure he's out.

We didn't say held back;
failed, we said *failed.*

*

August: the state fair.
An early start
before the crowds, car full,
mother driving, me
by the front window, you
and the boy cousins jostling
in the back seat, laughing, sun
shining on houses and houses
that are not ours, silver
runoff rain in curb gutters,
then: a gray mongrel,
ragged in the gutter, mouth
bleeding, water running
around him, his tail wagging,
rainbow spray of cars
passing, then me screaming
screaming until Mother
stops, annoyed, finds
the owner. You punching
me, shouting and shouting

Dope, you're making us late!
Stupid stupid dumb-ass girl!

The dog dying. Me sobbing.

*

I always put Walter
in his crate when I go out.
He's useless as a guard dog,
but his steel cage might fool
a thief into thinking he's vicious.
Thieves want the gentle ones
to sell as minnows
for pit bulls. Small dogs
get torn to bits in minutes,
but Walter would be just right—
big, gullible, curious, mystified
in the face of snarling evil—
before he realized the monster could kill him
he'd lie down in submission before it,
as you did.

*

Her family needing her
five dollars a week earnings,
after the eighth grade
she was put out to work
as a hired girl. Ever after
she considered herself
ignorant, uneducated,
especially before anyone
with a college degree.

Nevertheless, she called
for an appointment, dressed up,
drove into downtown Milwaukee.

Sometimes love risks its worst fear:

*Was it her fault? Was it because
she held him back in second grade?*

And sometimes mercy doesn't need to temper truth:

*No, not from one single thing,
not your fault, no one's fault.*

In her desk, a cache of clippings,
mostly my school awards.
Among the mementos, one
homemade Mother's Day card from him:

lightly penciled tentative cover,
drawing of a leafless gray tree, inside
the excruciating message:

from your retarded one.

*

Incomprehensible celebration—
always the first weekend in August,
parade, fireworks, talent show,
pancake breakfast, raffle, golf,
wiener roast—since 1976
Twinsville, Ohio has been cashing in
on what we fled.

International now, the duos,
triplets, quads, quints, identical, yes, even
fraternal, all dress alike.
One pair of fifty something sisters
share the same big black purse swinging
between them; two white haired ancients
harmonize with two harmonicas, blowing
through their identical dentures.

Almost never harmonious,
we each had our own birthday cake,
and we each got different presents
from the same grandparents, same parents,
always on the same inescapable day

*

When he outweighed me,
he had to move farther in.
I had to sit at the very end.

Up and down   up and down

the idea wasn't to balance—
Then where would we have gone?
Dangling your feet mid-air

you couldn't go anywhere—
the idea was to use your feet
to push up hard, make the other

come back down. But it was mean
if you were the down one, to just
jump off—then the up one drops down

in a tailbone-cracking crash
to the hard mud ground.
And then what? And then who?

*

It's a mistake to believe
one twin always knows
what the other is doing.

I don't know why
he drank himself to death
anymore than I know

what he was building
or destroying when he raised
that claw-foot hammer too far back.

We were ten, he had a Mohawk,
he was barefoot, shirtless.
From the back porch steps

I was watching him straddle
a two-by-four. He was yelling—
in a rage over what?—

when the claw-foot,
as if it had changed
its mind mid-swing,

swooped suddenly down
onto his skull,
then raked forward and up.

Why did he just stand there
silent, warm red rivers
already to his shoulders?

How was it I was watching?
That part I know—my job
was to run inside and tell.

*

Bang! Bang! You're dead.
Am not. Are so.

Mostly, I was the cop,
he, the robber or
I was the cowboy,
he, the Indian.
Thus, at the heart of it
I was the good one, he
the bad one, so why
all these years later,
did I consider a gun,
want to aim it straight
at my badge?

Bang! Bang! You're dead.
Am not. Am so.

*

Banker one; still can't balance
a checkbook one. Beautiful
wavy-haired one; your grandmother's
miserable hair one. Sturdy never
sick one; asthma eczema earache
high-fever bleeder always-got-
something one. Good sleeper one;
bed wetter. Pellet-gun pigeon
squirrel hunter one; stray runt
of the litter reject rescuer one.
Lots of friends one; loner.
Sharp dresser has girl friends
goes to the prom knows better
than to argue with adults one;
little commie pinko reads too many books
for her own good one. Never left
town or us one; leaver. David
named for your grandfather one;
Diane sounds good with David one.
First born male child; female.
Heart's pride; problem.
One who drank; one who didn't,
one who died; one who should have.

*

November: our birthday.
I would have you think
of me, if you could still
think, me outside at 3am
waiting for the puppy to pee.

I would have you know, if you could
still know, how he's a golden,
a good one, how already
he wants to retrieve everything,
even the moonlight silvering him
as he snuffles in the dry leaves.

And if you could still hear,
I would have you hear him
when I leave him
alone in his kitchen cage;
he whimpers, then howls—
for all the world like something human.

*

Finally you are first
and first forever
who were ever second—
ever delivered one hot half-hour after—
now you have surpassed me one full year:

first to lie alone stone still,
first to wear a mound of wilting bloom,
first to sink under the sour leaves,
first to freeze under the frozen snow,
first to molder, first to be mourned.

III

Little Thief

White winter sky blurring into white land,
heading home, west from Pittsburgh
on the flat track of the Ohio turnpike.
Aftermath of last week's blizzard:
still-buried corn fields, highway
wearing blinders of plowed drifts,
ice-crusted, cinder-splattered,
gray, slow to recede as grief.

Sunshine, road turning silver,
thin twinned electric tracks,
my brother's Lionel chugging
endless circles through cotton-batting,
the ever-winter of our childhood,
circle after circle, like the giant
windmachers sprinkled over wheat fields
in Denmark, huge white pylons topped
with huge white pinwheels turning
endless cartwheels, spinning
from the nothingness of wind
the strange current, fierce, underground
in cables stretching as far as Copenhagen.

A red Peterbilt blasts his horn, points
at my ridiculous pup sleeping sprawled,
paws up, sun-gold on the back seat,
sleeping the deep sleep all babies sleep.
Rumple of northern Indiana, car drawn
in the wake of the trucks: Angola,
Elkhart, South Bend, complication
of Chicago, 100 miles north to Milwaukee
and what is still home, last hour of daylight
throbbing tangerine sunset on my left shoulder.

*

When her short term memory went,
after the first hospitalization,
a meeting with the professionals
concerning "future living arrangements."

Carefully they laid it out:
the stove, the moldy food,
the unpaid bills, the busy road,
the forgotten medications.

"Assisted Living" they called it.
We sat around a dining room table
in the Family Conference Room,
she and I on one side, though
all she would say was

*Your brother would never
do this to me, never ever.*

*

One night I came home late—
hard to settle her or maybe
waiting for a nurse, meds—
The pup, too long in his crate,
wild to run. I unleashed him
on the empty asphalt parking lot
lit up behind the high school.

Late spring, warm showers
had poured a shallow black lake
glass smooth under the arc lights.

He charged into it possessed
with joy for his freedom
in the beloved element—
back and forth, back and forth—

From the shore I watched him run, leap
again and again until I understood
and ran too, leapt with him,
he barking in the ecstasy of it,
I soaked, laughing, weeping.

You were gone
and she was going
as the water flew living
liquid wind all around us.

*

Once, a gladness.
Perhaps turning your head
your smile when you saw me,

perhaps you were hunting,
when you came home,
when you set down your gun.

I've looked everywhere,
as if mislaid, but mine,
as something lost in my house

is still mine. Delight,
a place, a time, once,
perhaps we were fishing,

perhaps in a hushed voice
you told me where the trout lay,
or walking silently in the woods

you touched my arm,
pointed to where the deer sleep
in the deepest bracken. Memory,

from the Greek *mermera,*
to care for, which is to mourn,
to look for, to go down

underneath, to dive
as the sunken treasure hunter,
inside the barnacled tangle

for a gleam. Or to dig,
by feel to dig down, to ferret
inside the dark warren (ferret:

furittus, Latin, little thief),
by sound, by scent, finding once
a quivering, a softness.

*

World champions: he holds
his sister above his head
with one hand, twirling her,

her slender backbone in his palm,
her full weight pressing into
his muscled arm as she lets him

whirl her faster, lower her, lower,
lower, eyes closed, her head
four inches from the ice. Once

in Wisconsin-cold moonlight
we followed a black ribbon
of frozen river, skating out

onto Kellogg's swamp—windswept
ice so clear we were suspended
between two mirrored skies.

Scarves flying we are playing
crack the whip. I'm the one
on the end; the stars, the moon

are whirling, the world whirling,
do you understand, we're whirling
in wild cursive this little story

within our story. My brother holds
onto me with one hand. We're laughing,
he's yelling, *Hold on! Hold onto me!*

*

While I watched her die, pain rose up white
as a whistling swan, his rareness, that white.

Her face slipped from pink to ivory, piano keys
touched and touched, then a new music, blank sheet white.

Injured sparrow before the cat, her mind fell first,
then from the tired body ox, the ibis soul flew white.

I held her hand. No aura, no flash, nothing
like that. Nothing is black, never ever again is white.

A nurse came in, gentle, but intolerant of ambiguity:
no pulse, no heartbeat, and yes, eyes rolled white.

Each deathbed that terrible hospital white, my mother as
before, my brother. And you, me, will ours be this white?

Early October: the leaves were already down,
then down, down came snow's all-inclusive white.

She never saw her beloved again, her house,
though I did—its face scabbed, peeling, fading white.

Why black, why veiled, why opaque? As if grief
were solid. It's empty, lonely, without, white.

Thus I have her Danish porcelain, Royal Copenhagen,
not a single chip, hand-painted blue nosegays on bone white.

And when the swan is gone? Dickinson was right—
feathered—though after death, the feathers burn white.

Not the princess, not the huntress, not Diana,
Diane, her mother's sixty-year child in mourning white.

*

Morning was sunning the deck.
I was minding my own business,
pondering the idea of the soul

when two hummingbirds whizzed
out of nowhere and staged
a miniature dogfight.

My daughter once saw one ruby-throat
peck another one to death—
she took down her feeder,

but this time the loser
just buzzed back to base,
whatever base might be

for such a minute feathered engine.
It was the winner who surprised me—
fresh from his tiny victory,

he turned on me, *me*,
a sun-glassed Goliath! He whirred
straight over, eyed me steadily

(a cruel green eye in a slick green
helmet) as he throttled up
and threatened to lunge.

I wondered if he thought
I was a huge honeysuckle—
the mother-of-all fuchsias—

or whether it was folly, blind
compunction to puncture a giant
unknowable. It scared me—

that much I knew, and I jerked
my knee away from the menace,
real or imagined, I couldn't tell.

It was his presumption
I admired. In two seconds he was gone.
Whether it was two seconds

or someone's lifetime, your lifetime,
beyond goldenrod, gone.

*

Sometimes ghoulish—
as if tethered to a corpse—
as if a part of me were buried,
buried with him deep
in his mahogany coffin,
phantom limb aching
ghost who will not quiet.

Phantasm,
the worst part feeling as if
what's amputated is distorted,
shorter than before, contorted
into painful position. Treatment:
vibration, acupuncture, hypnosis,
biofeedback, often to little effect.
Keeping busy, focusing the attention
elsewhere most often prescribed.

Sometimes confusion—
sudden fluster, question
I cannot answer:
how many siblings do you have?

*

Last night I dreamed him prancing in the aquamarine,
my pup, who yesterday rolled frantically in the yard;
lined up on his back, three ticks, guts swollen
the size of grapes. I poisoned them; still

I had to turn, pull hard with tweezers
to get the embedded heads out.
The pup sat shivering in the sudsy insecticide;
he's a palomino now, honey-colored;

in the exuberant Caribbean surf
his extravagant tail flew it's feathered sail
luffed by the sea breeze. Honey-colored,
honey shot with sunlight.

*

Some poets want their tercets
to stay triplets, not expand
to quatrains, contract to couplets,

which might feel as if in the end
there was too much, too little,
a few too many, or too few words,

an uneasy imbalance that topples
the pyramid of a three-part
harmony. But I live twinned, unable

from conception to be apart
too far from some close half-other.
Think of how every heart

divides, needs each hollow chamber,
one side to fill, one to empty.
A missing line is my missing brother;

not until he was gone could I see
I was his not him, he was my not me.

*

They are dealing with the problem
of the homeless tastefully
at the Port Authority station
in New York City. Signs, bronze
with black letters advise:

> *Do not give money*
> *or food to the homeless;*
> *rest assured Social Services*
> *is aware of the problem and*
> *provides for their needs.*

Nonetheless, they beg,
dirty, stinking, sitting silent
against fluted marble columns.

My brother was never homeless.
He sat in an expensive black leather recliner,
dirty, stinking, silent, and no one,
not a one of us, could provide for him.

*

The presence of his absence,

as if I were Lakshmi Tatama, famous
little Indian girl born with four arms,
four legs, technically exhibiting
twin embolisation syndrome—
better known as *parasitic twins*—one
thriving in utero at the expense of the other
until the other melds into vestigial,
dependant, freak show material

as was Rudy Santos, Philippine *Octoman*,
one extra leg, three extra arms, undeveloped
head attached to his chest over his heart.

Lakshmi's parents opted for amputation
of the parasitic, a chance for normalcy,

but Rudy grew into adulthood,
rejected surgery, explaining to reporters
he was attached to the extra, couldn't
imagine himself without it.

*

Shack of hair and bone—
where will I find you now?
DNA would say you are still
you, as a place is still a place
even abandoned into ghost town.

Shall I say the soul leaves behind
the body's company house, say sorrow
makes a nightly round, rattles
the doors, says no one, no one
ever really believes the gold
will give out, and how long,
how long you've already been gone.

*

Inside of her
I could not tell
where he, one soft side,

left off, and I,
the other half, began.
Curled back to back

we made a butterfly.
There was never a picture
of it; with her body

she grew that picture
inside each of us.
After she found him

where he had fallen,
and after he died,
she taped the first photo

by the phone,
the hospital snapshot
of her propped up,

young face tentative,
smiling, a sleeping full moon
on each winged arm.

Long ago she wrote my name
with an arrow to one
dark-haired circle,

his name on a thin line
to the other. Now,
she hasn't taped it well;

again it's fallen
to the kitchen floor—
She's not smiling at either

of us in the snapshot;
she's smiling straight ahead
saying, *Look,*

this one is you, this one is your brother.

Epilogue

Years, light years
of the heart ago, at night
my brother and I walked
through deep snow going
to feed the chickens.

My brother carried the lantern.
In the yellow light,
its own shadow made a little ark
bobbing across a white ocean
of snowy yard.

Fifteen years now he's lain
in darkness.
No, no, not so—
across the page I carry the lantern.

Why do you think you were
called to this world?
...You were called to be loved
You were called when you weren't here—

"Empty Shadow"
—Brenda Hillman

David,
It's 2012, a rare gift of November
generosity: 65 degrees in New York city!
With a bunch other tourists
I am sitting in Friday evening twilight
on the steps to the Metropolitan.

It's our birthday—we are 70!

Down front on the sidewalk
a lone saxophonist, lost
in his solo song to the city,
raises his riff up over the taxis
in a deep ribbon of sweetness that floats

high above the avenue reaching
all the way to Times Square.
Throng swirling, light everywhere,
buskers flip and somersault in the street,
Minnie and Mickey mingle, working the crowd,
the Cat in the Hat ambles by.
On a traffic island, a guy in cowboy boots
and his underpants
sings and plays his guitar. Two Statues

of Liberty: one in a rainbow bikini
lifts her rainbow-lighted torch; the other,
silver spray-painted head to toe,
sits on the curb, eating a corn dog.

David, we've elected a black president! Twice!

And since you've been gone,
everyone has their own computer and look—
we all have these little portable phones—
you can call anyone from anywhere.

Nearly dark now, come with me
into the great museum; we'll go
past the complicated first floor armor,
past the second floor Andy Warhol retrospective
soup cans, Marilyns and Jackies,
past the third floor *Buddhism*
and the Silk Road Special Exhibit
peace and a thousand Bodhisattvas.

Here, before this single lighted case, we'll stop
for Han Dynasty funerary miniatures,
Fisher Price toys from the third century,
little moss green ceramic models of everything
needed. I would send them all with you.
I would gather the small pen with six rams, the one
with four sleek geese, the one with three stout pigs.
I would give you the granary tower, the sturdy
outdoor oven, the many storied watchtower,
give you the family house and its courtyard,
the well and its fragile bucket.

CPSIA information can be obtained at www.ICGtesting.com
Printed in the USA
BVOW08s1611170515

400494BV00001B/16/P